Bonsai Trees for Beginners

A Beginner's Guide to Cultivating and Nurturing Your Own Bonsai Tree

By: Hiro Nakamura

Text Copyright © Lightbulb Publishing

All rights reserved. No part of this guide may be reproduced in any form without permission in writing from the publisher except in the case of brief quotations embodied in critical articles or reviews.

Legal & Disclaimer

The information in this book and its contents are not designed to replace or substitute any form of medical or professional advice. It is not intended to replace the need for independent medical, financial, legal, or other professional advice or services as may be required. The content and information in this book have been provided for educational and entertainment purposes only.

The content and information in this book have been compiled from reliable sources and are accurate to the best of the Author's knowledge, information, and belief. However, the Author cannot guarantee the accuracy and validity and cannot be held liable for errors and/or omissions. Furthermore, changes are made periodically to this book as and when needed.

Where appropriate and/or necessary, you must consult a professional (including but not limited to your doctor, attorney, financial advisor, or such other professional advisor) before using any of the suggested remedies, techniques, or information in this book.

Upon using the contents and information in this book, you agree to hold harmless the Author from and against any damages, costs, and expenses, including any legal fees potentially resulting from the application of any of the information provided. This disclaimer applies to any loss, damages, or injury caused by the use and application, whether directly or indirectly, of any advice or information presented, whether for breach of contract, tort, negligence, personal injury, criminal intent, or under any other cause of action.

You agree to accept all the risks of using the information presented in this book.

You agree by continuing to read this book that, where appropriate and/or necessary, you shall consult a professional (including but not limited to your doctor, attorney, financial advisor, or such other advisor as needed) before using any of the suggested remedies, techniques, or information in this book.

Table of Contents

Chapter 1: Introduction 1
    A - What is the art of Bonsai? 1
    B - History and origin of Bonsai 2
    C - Why do you need Bonsai? 4
    D - Is Bonsai the same as Punsai 5

Chapter 2: Styles of Bonsai (with recommended containers) ... 7
    A - Formal Upright (Chokkan) 7
    B - Informal Upright (Moyogi) 8
    C - Slanting (Shakan) 9
    D - Windswept (Fukinagashi) 9

Chapter 3: Bonsai styles and how to care for them 11
    A - Formal Upright Bonsai 11
    B - Informal Upright Bonsai 11
    C - Slanting Bonsai 12
    D - Windswept bonsai 12

Chapter 4: Required Tools for bonsai care 15
    A - Pruning shears 15
    B - Concave cutter 16
    C - Knob cutter 16
    D - Wire Pliers and wire cutter 16
    E - Tools for bonsai root care 17

Chapter 5: Growing and Cultivating Techniques 19
    A - Potting 19
    B - Repotting 21
    C - Wiring and Shaping 22

D - Pruning, Trimming.. 23
Chapter 6: Starting to grow your bonsai tree........................... 25
A - Selecting the right Bonsai Tree for you............................... 25
B - Select the Pot... 28
C - Choice of Soil and Fertilizer.. 29
D - Cultivating the perfect growing environment................... 32
E - Preparing yourself and the space....................................... 33
Chapter 7: Maintenance Techniques to Keep the Bonsai Tree Happy.. 35
A - Watering, Fertilizing, Repotting... 35
Chapter 8: Display and Decorating 37
A. Aesthetics and Styles... 37
Chapter 9: Caring for your Bonsai tree according to seasons and climate... 39
Chapter 10: Pest, Diseases, and Fungus Control 41
A - How to avoid them (using alcohol, neem oil, pesticides, and insecticides) 42
B - Dealing with different types of Pests................................. 43
Chapter 11: Techniques and Strategies to grow Bonsai trees. 45
Chapter 12: Additional Information 47
A - Famous Bonsai Artists in the World.................................. 48
B - Oldest Bonsai Tree... 49
Chapter 13: Conclusion.. 53
Chapter 14: Glossary... 55

Chapter 1

Introduction

The word Bonsai originates from two Japanese words: **Bon** or "**tray or Bowl**," meaning small, and Sai or "plant" or "tree," which means **"A tree planted in a container or a tray"** or "A tree planted by hand."

A - What is the art of Bonsai?

Bonsai is the art of growing various trees and shrubs in small, shallow containers by careful and precise training and pruning, that the plant is shaped and manipulated to give the appearance of an older, mature tree. The shape of the tree changes to more closely resemble how a tree might seem when growing naturally. It requires calm patience, careful consideration of every aspect, and deliberate activity to form a growing tree or shrub over a period of years. To maintain bonsai trees, many different methods are used, including grafting, wiring, clipping, and pinching.

Actually, bonsai is a traditional Japanese practice of pruning and training miniature trees to grow in a small pot. The art of bonsai is a traditional Japanese Art. Various types of trees are carefully trained to grow into small trees or toys. In Japan, there is a long history of the cultivation of bonsai since the first century. Bonsai comes from Japan but can be traced back thousands of years and probably originated in China. The art is a tribute to nature and produces stunning miniature trees and shrubs in gardens and parks that take your breath away.

B - History and origin of Bonsai

Although the word 'Bonsai' is Japanese. However, bonsai art originated in the Chinese empire. Chinese traditionally referred to bonsai trees using the words "punsai" or "penjing." In Chinese, the word "Pen" is meant for pot, while "Jing" is for scenery or a landscape. Since 700 AD, the Chinese have been practicing the art of "pun-sai," which involves adopting unique methods to produce dwarf plants and trees in containers.

Growing miniature trees and bushes was first conceived in China 2300 years ago. Two ladies showed presenting miniature rockeries with tiny plants in small bowls in the tomb paintings for Crown Prince Zhang Huai from the year 706 AD. The oldest documented descriptions of these pun wan - tray toys date from this era. The art had somewhat matured. It is said that twisted and oddly shaped examples from the wild were the first trees to be captured and then placed in containers. Because the trees could not be used for any practical, everyday uses, such as timber, they were considered "holy."

Several regional styles would evolve over time in the different nations with many diverse landscapes; porcelain containers exhibited on wooden platforms would give way to earthenware and ceramic ones. Likewise, a number of attempts would be made to shape the trees using bamboo frames, brass wire, or lead strips. Numerous artists featured a miniaturized potted tree as a sign of a cultured man's lifestyle. They were referred to as pun-sai or "tray planting" after the 16th century.

Introduction

In Japan, the oldest tray landscapes are said to have been imported from China at least 1200 years ago (as religious souvenirs). Its shape and style don't have the capacity to move unless it is maintained by people who craft it with loving care. Generally, Japanese pots were deeper than those from the mainland. The resulting gardening form was called Hachi-Noki, literally, the bowl's tree. A folktale from the late 1300s, about an impoverished samurai who sacrificed his last three dwarf potted trees to provide warmth for a traveling monk on a cold winter night, became popular. In Japan, miniature trees weren't originally revealed in graphic detail until around 8000 years ago. Chinese culture captivated the Japanese. During the decades, images from the narrative were reproduced in many media, including woodblock prints.

In the West during 1604, there was a description in Spanish of how Chinese immigrants in the tropical islands of the Philippines were growing small Ficus trees onto hand-sized pieces of coral. In China/Macau, the earliest-known English sighting of miniature potted trees (root in a pan) dates to 1637. reports in the following century, including from Japan. The Philadelphia Exposition in 1876, the Paris Expositions in 1878 and 1889, the Chicago Expo in 1893, the St. Louis World's Fair in 1904, the Japan-Britain Exhibition in 1910, and the San Francisco Exposition in 1915. All included Japanese dwarf trees.

The first book about Japanese dwarf trees to be written wholly in a European language was published in French in 1902, followed by an English translation in 1940. Miniature Trees and Landscapes by Yoshimura and Halford was released in 1957. Yuji Yoshimura served as the direct link between Japanese Classical Bonsai art and the forward-thinking Western approach, resulting in an attractive, tasteful adaptation for the modern world, and it would come to be recognized as the "Bible of Bonsai in the West." In order to further emphasize the utilization of indigenous materials, John Naka from California expanded this sharing by imparting knowledge both personally and in writing, first in the US and subsequently globally.

During this time, **Saikei**, a type of Japanese landscape, and **Penjing**, a type of Chinese revival, were being imported to the West. Countless tree compositions grew to be regarded and acknowledged as authentic creations.

C - Why do you need Bonsai?

If you love the idea of decorating your space with beautiful, pleasant miniature plants and don't want to spend a fortune on them, then Bonsai trees are the best option for you. Bonsai is a living artwork that can be used to beautify the entrance of your house, the garden, or the public square. Simply a small tree in a pot is considered one of the most popular home shrubs and trees nowadays.

There are many reasons to start your own bonsai tree. Firstly, people all over the world want to own one of these diminutive living entities for different uses, like keeping them as a companion, others as display trees, or wanting their own bonsai collectibles. Secondly, Bonsai trees can be used in your yard, backyard, or garden to create a space that catches the eye while relaxing the mind.

Introduction

D - Is Bonsai the same as Punsai

The art of growing dwarf or miniature shrubs and trees in containers is related to both terms, "Bonsai" and "Punsai ."The term bonsai represents the Japanese art of growing trees in pots, while the reverse was used by the Chinese. Despite the terminology, penjing or punsai is based on more focused on the artistic interpretation of natural phenomena, whereas bonsai is more disciplined in technical skill to grow plants and is a more refined, stylistic depiction of nature (when showing a single tree). Usually, penjing symbolizes miniature landscapes, displaying a combination of rocks, trees, and figures, although single plants showed in China art. The main difference between them is the method used to grow trees and shrubs.

The Japanese bonsai is a version of the original traditional Chinese art form called penjing. Unlike Penzai, which utilizes old-fashioned techniques to produce entire natural scenery in small pots that mimic large-scale and realistic landscapes, Japanese bonsai is more simple and more natural.

Chapter 2

Styles of Bonsai (with recommended containers)

A variety of styles to classify bonsai trees have evolved with time based on soil conditions and the natural environment of the location. Trees don't necessarily need to follow any certain form because the aesthetics are free to individual interpretation and imagination.

The various bonsai styles, however, should be used as basic instructions for various shapes and must act as guidelines for beginners to train miniature trees within a pot.

Bonsai Styles

4 Main Types of Bonsai Trees

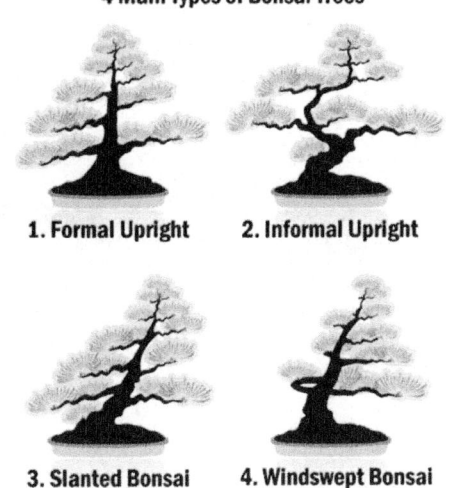

1. Formal Upright
2. Informal Upright
3. Slanted Bonsai
4. Windswept Bonsai

A - Formal Upright (Chokkan)

A formal upright bonsai tree is a very common style of bonsai. It is characterized by a main trunk that grows straight up from the soil and becomes thinner toward the top. The main characters are:

- Frequently exist naturally when exposed to plenty of sunlight.

- The main truck must be thicker at the bottom and gets thinner with the increase in height.

- Branching should grow at around one-fourth of the trunk's overall length.

- A single branch should make up the tree's crown.

- Usually, a rectangular container is used for this style.

B - Informal Upright (Moyogi)

An informal upright bonsai tree is characterized as growing upright, but the trunk may zig-zag a little on its way up. This style also occurs both naturally and art of bonsai with a rectangular shaped container. Main features are

- The main trunk grows upright approximately in the shape of the letter 'S.'

- A clearly visible tapering of the trunk.

- Evenly spaced branches along the entire length of the trunk.

- There are no large bends in the trunk, which results in an open appearance.

- The truck has only subtle curves.

Styles of Bonsai (with recommended containers)

C - Slanting (Shakan)

A slanting bonsai tree grows in a leaning direction (more than 45 degrees from the base), probably when a tree grows under a shadow and must bend toward sunlight. Its main features are:

- The tree leans in one direction at an angle of 60- 80 degrees from the ground.
- The first branch grows opposite the leaning direction of the tree in order to create a sense of visual balance.
- The truck must be thicker at the base compared to the top.
- A circular-shaped container is mostly used for slanting bonsai style.

D - Windswept (Fukinagashi)

Windswept bonsai, all the branches grow in one direction giving an appearance of a sail as if the wind is blowing the tree constantly in one direction. The main attributes are:

- Windswept bonsai is similar to leaning bonsai.
- All branches of the tree grow in one direction (right or left side of the truck).
- Generally, a rectangular truck is used for windswept style.

Source:
https://www.bonsaiempire.com/
https://www.homestratosphere.com/pictures-bonsai-trees/
https://youtu.be/rhYH1mA3Wv0

Chapter 3

Bonsai styles and how to care for them

A - Formal Upright Bonsai

A most classical and generic style among various styles of bonsai, upright bonsai. Usually, it has a cone form with symmetrical branches. In order to maintain a natural bonsai style, you must follow particular guidelines

- Don't put the plant at the center of the container but at the right or left side of the container.

- A tapering truck may be shaped by regular pruning top-down, making the lower branches grow larger and thicker.

- To achieve a consistent space between the branches, you must trim small branches from the lower portion of the tree's truck.

B - Informal Upright Bonsai

The present bonsai style is less formal and a variant of the formal upright bonsai style. The informal upright style has a dense cone with an asymmetrical truck. The following care guide must be adopted to maintain this bonsai style.

- The roots of the bonsai are trained to grow forward towards the front of the pot in order to maintain an asymmetrical truck.

- Usually, branches start to grow approximately 1/3 of the way up the trunk. Likewise, in the formal upright and lower branches are pruned regularly.

- Develop the crown with dense twigs and branches.
- Regular watering and fertilization are needed during the early growth of the trunk.

C - Slanting Bonsai

Naturally, trees grow slanted if they have only a single way to get sunlight, generally in thick, dense forests. To create a slanted style, beginners need to do careful guidelines.

- You may either slant the pot so that the tree goes slanted by wiring.
- By limiting the direction of daily sunlight, the tree grows in that specific direction during early growth.
- Generally, the roots of a slanted tree grow outwards in the opposite direction to balance the gravitational forces. You must use hard soil (clayey soils) and watering points to support the roots.

D - Windswept bonsai

A rare bonsai style that is hard to develop due to the skill and time needed. Naturally, windswept bonsai style is produced when exposed to the cold seasonal wind that damages the buds of one side of the tree and encourages branch growth in the direction of the wind, particularly in the mountain and coastal areas. To cultivate it, you need to manifest following guidelines.

- Choose a tree with a firm foundation and with more growth on one side and often very few branches on the other side.

Bonsai styles and how to care for them

- Tree trunk must be "off center" while the branches point towards the open area.
- The sprout or buds growing in the opposite direction of the wind must be removed regularly.

Note: During the early growth stages, all bonsai styles must be fertilized and watered on a regular basis.

Chapter 4

Required Tools for bonsai care

For beginners to care for bonsai, the training, and maintenance need the use of the right tools. You must be able to cut the trees precisely, with a certain profile, and with smooth, even edges. It is ideal for novices to start off with a few basic tools, such as a good concave cutter and a regular shear. Later on, you will require more specialized instruments the more intensively you deal with bonsai.

A wide variety of tools we can add to our toolkit, including shears, cutters, pliers, saws, and special tools for repotting. Let's take a closer look at these categories of Bonsai tools.

A - Pruning shears

Shears are meant for cutting twigs, smaller branches, leaves, or roots (wilted or damaged) in order to trim and reshape the tree.

B - Concave cutter

For bonsai trees, concave cutters are perfect for trimming living or dead branches leaving stretched wounds, and those wounds heal very fast with very few scars.

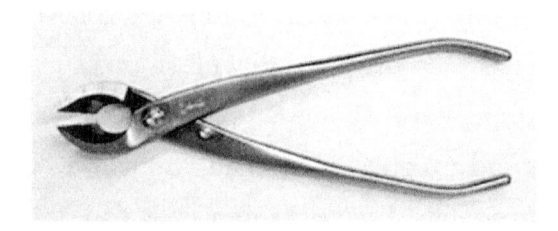

C - Knob cutter

Knob cutters are perfect for pruning branches, and it leaves a spherical cut on the branch, thereby allowing it to heal flush with the surface.

D - Wire Pliers and wire cutter

Bonsai wire pliers are perfect for bending wire around branches while wiring your tree. The rounded ends help ensure that your tree does not become damaged during the process. Also can be used for stripping the bark and fiber of your bonsai in order to give it an aged, weathered look.

Required Tools for bonsai care

While wiring your bonsai, wire cutters are employed to cut the wire to the desired length.

E - Tools for bonsai root care

In order to care for bonsai tree roots, beginners may use Root cutters, hooks, and rakes. Root hooks and root rakes, available in different sizes with 1-3 teeth, are commonly meant for opening the rootball and carefully combing the roots, and removing old soil between the roots during repotting.

Chapter 5

Growing and Cultivating Techniques (or Grooming Your Bonsai Tree)

Maintaining the structure and growth of your bonsai is important for you. The care and management of your bonsai tree is not a hard task. However, it may take your time and management skills. Most significantly, it requires proper pruning, trimming, and watering of your bonsai tree as well as its potting and repotting techniques. Here we will discuss all the necessary skills and techniques to cultivate and grow your bonsai in ways that give you pleasure and aesthetic value.

The type of care needed for the growing and cultivation of bonsai depends on the kind of bonsai you want to grow for indoor and outdoor purposes because deciduous and coniferous bonsai types have different growth requirements for soil as the growing medium, moisture, fertilizer use, as well as maintenance requirements like wiring and how frequently to prune and trim.

A - Potting

Actually, many containers can serve as a pot for a bonsai tree. Potting for the first time your bonsai, you must keep in mind some requirements, including drainage holes for draining irrigation water and wiring holes so that the tree can be fixed to the pot. When looking for a pot, the most important thing to keep in mind is the required measurement, particularly the height, and depth of the pot according to your chosen bonsai tree type.

The pot should be of the same height as the trunk is wide above the surface roots (Nebari). Oval and rectangular pots are usually 2/3 of the tree's height. Round or square pots are 1/3 the height of the tree.

Ceramic, concrete, plastics, and certain metals (metals may release toxins) based pots may be used. But a classic bonsai pot is made of ceramic or porcelain, and it is stoneware burned, which means that it absorbs and holds no water in the material, which is important for the tree's health.

Pot can be prepared by cutting square or rectangular pieces of mesh that are just slightly bigger than each hole and placing them over the holes. If you have many holes in a row, you might find it easier to use larger pieces of the mesh according to the size of your pot. The next step is to cut a long piece of wire that will enter from the bottom of the pot through two drainage holes (farthest away from each other). This wire is called the anchorage wire used to secure the roots of the tree.

Growing and Cultivating Techniques (or Grooming Your Bonsai Tree)

B - Repotting

How often you should repot depends on the size of the pot and tree species of your Bonsai. Fast-growing trees need to be repotted every two years, sometimes sooner. Older, more mature trees need to be repotted every three to five years. Repotting is not something that should be routine. Check your Bonsai early in the spring by carefully removing the tree from its pot. If you see the roots circling around the root system, your Bonsai needs to be repotted. If the roots are still contained within the soil, leave it and check the following spring again.

Early spring is the best time to repot your bonsai trees as they are still dormant, not sustaining full-grown foliage, and the buds begin to swell. At this stage, minimum damaging effects occur during repotting. Repotting in early spring will also ensure that damage done to the root system will be quickly repaired as soon as the tree starts growing. Some tree species can also be repotted in fall but never repot a bonsai in summer or winter.

C - Wiring and Shaping

A very important technique used to train and style Bonsai trees is wiring. By wrapping wire around the branches of a tree, you can bend and reposition the branches to your liking. It takes a few months before the branches are set in their new position. Most tree species can be wired at any time of the year. Deciduous trees however are much easier to wire in late winter due to the absence of leaves. Be attentive when applying wire during the growing season, as branches grow thick quite fast, which can result in ugly scars from the wire cutting into the bark.

i) Wire Size

Wire is available in sizes from 1-8mm thick (gauges 20 to 2). There is no need to purchase every available wire gauge. We suggest starting with; 1, 1.5, 2.5, and 4 mm thick wires. When wiring thick branches, it is recommended to wrap them with raffia (a palm fiber) soaked in water to protect the branches from being damaged by the wire when shaping.

ii) Working with wires

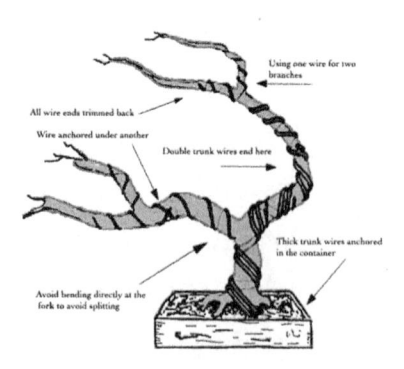

Firstly, wire two branches of similar thickness near each other using a single piece of wire. This technique is known as 'double-wiring,' and it prov ides more support for both branches. The remaining branches should be wired separately. Make sure to wire all the branches you intend on shaping before actually bending them. When wiring an entire Bonsai tree, start working from the trunk to the primary branches and then wiring the secondary branches. As a rule of thumb, use wires that are 1/3 of the thickness of the branch you are wiring. The wire should be thick enough to hold the branch in its new position.

D - Pruning, Trimming

Trees have a natural tendency to grow with apical dominance. This means that the main, central stem of the plant grows more dominantly than its side stems. For example, on a branch, the main stem of the branch is more dominant over its side twigs. This natural mechanism encourages trees to grow higher to prevent them from being shaded out by competing trees. By distributing growth to the top and outer edges, the tree's inner and lower branches will eventually die, while the top branches grow out of proportion, both of which are not desirable traits for Bonsai aesthetics.

Generally, the best time to structure-prune a tree is in the early spring and some cases, late autumn, just before and after the growing season. The exact timing differs from species to species. Start pruning by removing all the dead branches from the tree. Once that's done, take a close look at your tree and decide which branches need to be removed to create your desired design. Pruning thick branches typically results in ugly scars, but by using special concave cutters, you can reduce scaring effects significantly. We've provided a few guidelines in the image below, but designing your tree is more of a creative process and not something bound by rules.

Chapter 6

Starting to grow your bonsai tree

Bonsai is a Japanese art form that involves growing and shaping miniature trees in pots or trays. Bonsai art aims to create an aesthetically pleasing and balanced composition that resembles a mature tree in nature but on a small scale. Such trees are trained and pruned over time to maintain their size and shape, and they are often displayed, along with other decorative elements, in a carefully arranged setting.

A - Selecting the right Bonsai Tree for you

Getting started with bonsai can be a fun and rewarding experience. Start with a species that is hardy, easy to grow, and adaptable to the bonsai training techniques. Some popular species for beginners include **Chinese Elm, Ficus, and Juniper**. Bonsai trees need proper light, water, fertilizer, and soil. Make sure to research the specific needs of the species you have chosen and adjust accordingly. Pruning, wiring, and repotting are the main techniques used to shape and maintain bonsai trees. Start with basic pruning, and work your way up to more advanced techniques as you gain experience. Remember, bonsai is an art form that takes time, patience, and practice to master. Enjoy the process, and don't be afraid to make mistakes – they are all part of the learning experience.

i. Best Bonsai for Beginners

For beginners, the best bonsai trees are those that are hardy, easy to grow, and adaptable to the bonsai training techniques. Here are some popular bonsai species that are well-suited for beginners:

a) Japanese white pine,

b) Japanese Maple, and

c) Chinese elm

a - Japanese white pine (*Pinus parviflora*)

The Japanese White Pine is a specie of pine tree that is often used in bonsai cultivation. It is known for its attractive, blue-green needles and unique bark that becomes more gnarled and interesting with age. This species is also tolerant to harsh growing conditions and can be trained into a variety of bonsai styles, including formal upright, slanting, and windswept. Growing this specie requires a bit of patience, as this species grows slowly. However, with proper care and attention, it can be a stunning and long-lasting addition to any bonsai collection.

b - Japanese Maple (*Acer palmatum*)

The Japanese Maple is native to Japan and is a popular species for bonsai cultivation due to its graceful branches and stunning fall color. This species is known for its ability to adapt to a wide range of growing conditions. There are many different varieties of Japanese Maple, each with its own unique features, including different leaf shapes, sizes, and colors. Some popular varieties of bonsai include the **Bloodgood, Osakazuki,** and **Sango-Kaku**. Some varieties of Japanese Maple are hardier than others, so it's important to choose a variety that is well-suited to your local climate and growing conditions. If you're interested in growing a Japanese Maple bonsai, it's recommended to seek out guidance from experienced bonsai artists and learn as much as possible about the specific care requirements of this species and the variety you have chosen.

c - Chinese Elm (*Ulmus parvifolia*)

The Chinese Elm is a popular species for bonsai cultivation due to its attractive leaves, delicate bark, and ability to adapt to a wide range of growing conditions. This species is native to Asia and is known for its tolerance of pruning and shaping, making it a great choice for bonsai enthusiasts of all levels of experience. Some important care considerations for this species include providing adequate light and water, avoiding excessive fertilizer, and protecting it from pests and disease. Chinese Elm bonsai can be trained into a variety of styles, including formal upright, slanting, windswept, and cascade, depending on the desired look and effect. This species is also versatile in terms of its location, as it can be grown both indoors and outdoors.

B - Select the Pot

The pot selection for a bonsai is an important factor in its overall appearance and health. The pot should be proportional to the size of the bonsai, with enough room for the roots to spread but not so large that it overwhelms the tree. Pots for bonsai are typically made of either ceramic or plastic, with ceramic being the more traditional option. Ceramic pots come in a variety of colors, shapes, and sizes, while plastic pots are lighter and less fragile. Bonsai need good drainage to prevent root rot, so it's important to choose a pot with adequate drainage holes and to make sure there is enough space between the bottom of the pot and the soil to allow excess water to drain away.

The pot should complement the style of the bonsai and enhance its overall appearance. For example, a formal upright bonsai may look best in a square or rectangular pot, while a windswept bonsai may look better in a round or oval pot. The color of the pot can also be important in terms of its impact on the overall appearance of the bonsai. Dark pots can make a bonsai appear heavier, while lighter pots can make it appear lighter and more delicate. Ultimately, the pot selection for a bonsai is a matter of personal taste, and the best pot for your bonsai will depend on the tree's size, style, and individual requirements. When in doubt, it's always a good idea to seek the advice of an experienced bonsai artist.

C - Choice of Soil and Fertilizer

The type of soil selected for a bonsai is critical to its health and growth. Bonsai trees need well-draining soil that allows water to drain away quickly in order to prevent root rot, and their roots need air to thrive, so the soil used should be light and airy to ensure good aeration and well drainage. For example, coarse-textured sandy soil helps to improve drainage and aeration, which is important for bonsai roots. A mix of coarse sand, akadama (volcanic soil with coarse, crumbly texture), pumice (Soils with porous, lightweight texture with good drainage and aeration), and perlite (a volcanic rock that has been expanded and crushed to create a lightweight, porous soil texture with excellent drainage and aeration), can provide the best combination of drainage, aeration, and nutrient retention for most bonsai species. The soil should retain enough nutrients to feed the bonsai but not so much that it stays waterlogged, which can lead to root rot. So, the soil could be enriched by organic matter, such as compost or well-rotted manure, to provide additional nutrients. Bonsai prefer slightly acidic soil with a pH between 6 and 7. It's important to note that different species of bonsai may have different soil requirements, so it's a good idea to research the specific needs of your tree before choosing a soil type. In general, a soil texture that is well-draining, lightweight, and porous is ideal for bonsai cultivation.

Another important aspect of bonsai cultivation is to provide the necessary nutrients for healthy growth and development. Bonsai species need a balanced combination of nutrients, including nitrogen, phosphorus, and potassium, as well as trace elements, such as iron, magnesium, and zinc. When looking for fertilizer, you must ensure that it provides a balanced combination of these nutrients. Bonsai fertilizers come in different formulas, such as granular, liquid, and slow-release. Choose a formula that is convenient for your growing conditions and schedule. The frequency of fertilizing will depend on the species of bonsai, the growing conditions, and the time of year. Some bonsai may need to be fertilized monthly, while others may only need to be fertilized once or twice a year. Organic fertilizers, such as compost or fish emulsion, provide slow-release nutrients and are more environmentally friendly. Synthetic fertilizers are typically more concentrated and provide faster results, but they may also be more damaging to the environment. Some species of bonsai may have specific fertilizer requirements, so it's important to research the specific needs of your tree before choosing a fertilizer.

In general, a balanced fertilizer that provides a combination of nutrients and is formulated for the specific species of bonsai you are growing is a good choice. Deciduous bonsai, such as Maple or elm, typically need to be fertilized during their growing season, which is usually from spring to fall. During the early growth period, young bonsai trees have a higher demand for nutrients and should be fertilized every 2-4 weeks more frequently than mature trees, and adjust the frequency based on the growth and health of the tree. Stop fertilizing when the leaves begin to fall. While coniferous bonsai, such as pine or juniper, typically need to be fertilized less frequently than deciduous species. They may only need to be fertilized once or twice a year, usually in spring and early summer.

Slow-release fertilizers can provide a long-lasting source of nutrients and can reduce the need for frequent fertilizing. Repotting is also a good opportunity to fertilize bonsai, as it provides the roots with fresh soil and nutrients. In general, it's important to monitor the growth and health of your bonsai and adjust the frequency of fertilizing based on its needs. Over-fertilizing can be harmful to the health of the tree, so it's important to follow the manufacturer's recommendations.

D - Cultivating the perfect growing environment

Growing conditions are critical to the success of bonsai cultivation. Bonsai need bright but indirect sunlight to grow healthy and strong. Most species of bonsai will grow well in a sunny location with protection from the hottest part of the day. Bonsai prefer to grow in temperatures between 60-75°F. Some species can tolerate temperatures outside this range, but it's important to research the specific needs of your bonsai and provide a suitable growing environment. Bonsai are native to regions with high humidity, so it's important to provide adequate humidity for your bonsai. This can be done by misting the leaves regularly, providing a tray of water near the bonsai, or using a humidifier.

Bonsai species also need well-draining soil that contains a mix of organic material and minerals. The soil should be loose and aerated to allow for proper root development and need consistent watering to prevent drought stress. The frequency of watering will depend on the species of bonsai, the size of the pot, and the growing conditions. It's important to monitor the soil moisture level regularly and adjust the watering schedule as needed. Regular pruning and training are essential for shaping and maintaining the size of your bonsai. Research the specific needs of your bonsai and follow the pruning and training guidelines for your species. By providing optimal growing conditions, including adequate light, temperature, humidity, soil, watering, and pruning, you can help your bonsai thrive and achieve its full potential.

E - Preparing yourself and the space

Bonsai offers many benefits that connect human beings in meaningful ways. It has a deep connection with human beings and has been cultivated for centuries for its beauty, tranquility, and spiritual benefits. Cultivating bonsai can be a meditative and calming experience. It requires patience, attention to detail, and a focus on the present moment, which can help reduce stress and improve overall well-being. Bonsai provides an outlet for creative expression and allows individuals to express their individuality through the design and shaping of their trees. Bonsai provides an opportunity to bring the beauty of nature indoors and appreciate the majesty of trees in miniature form. It can help people connect with nature and appreciate the intricate and delicate ecosystem balance. Bonsai has a rich cultural history, with roots in ancient China and Japan, and has been passed down from generation to generation. Cultivating bonsai can connect individuals with their cultural heritage and provide a connection to their ancestors. Bonsai provides an opportunity to learn about the biology and ecology of trees and their role in the ecosystem. It can also teach important skills such as pruning, wiring, and soil management, which can be applied to other areas of life.

Whether it's through mindfulness, creativity, connection with nature, tradition, or education, bonsai provides an enriching and rewarding experience that can improve our lives in many ways. The best place to keep bonsai depends on the species and its specific growing requirements. However, most bonsai species require bright but indirect sunlight. A location near a window that provides bright, filtered light for several hours a day is ideal. Avoid exposing your bonsai to direct, intense sun for extended periods of time, as this can damage the leaves and cause the tree to become stressed. If you have species that require different temperature ranges, make sure to provide them with the conditions they need. Avoid exposing your bonsai to extreme temperatures, as this can cause stress and damage. Bonsai prefer to grow in environments with high humidity. If your home has low humidity, you can provide additional humidity by regularly misting the leaves or placing a tray of water near the bonsai. Make sure your bonsai is protected from harsh winds and other environmental hazards that can cause damage or stress. Bonsai can be displayed in many different ways, including on shelves, in a corner, or as a centerpiece on a table. Choose a location that allows you to enjoy your bonsai and provides it with the conditions it needs to thrive.

Chapter 7

Maintenance Techniques to Keep the Bonsai Tree Happy

A - Watering, Fertilizing, Repotting

Maintaining a bonsai involves regular care and attention to ensure that it stays healthy, beautiful, and true to its intended style. Bonsai need to be watered regularly to maintain the health of their roots. However, too much watering causes root rot. The frequency of watering will depend on the species, the size of the pot, the type of soil, and the ambient temperature and humidity. Be sure to water your bonsai thoroughly, and make sure that the soil does not dry out completely.

Regular pruning is important to maintain the shape and style of your bonsai. This involves removing unwanted or excessive growth, including leaves, branches, and roots. The timing and frequency of pruning will depend on the species, but most bonsai benefit from regular maintenance pruning throughout the year. Wiring is a technique used to shape and train bonsai into specific styles. Wiring involves wrapping a wire around the branches and trunk of the tree to guide its growth in the desired direction. The wire should be checked regularly and removed once the desired shape is achieved.

Regular fertilizing is important to provide your bonsai with the nutrients it needs to grow and remain healthy. The type of fertilizer and frequency of application will depend on the species, but most bonsai benefit from regular applications of balanced fertilizer throughout the growing season. Bonsai need to be repotted periodically to provide them with fresh soil, remove any roots that have become cramped, and accommodate growth. The timing and frequency of repotting will depend on the species, but most bonsai benefit from repotting every 2-3 years. By performing these regular maintenance tasks, you can ensure that your bonsai remains healthy and beautiful and continues to provide you with enjoyment for years to come.

Chapter 8

Display and Decorating

A. Aesthetics and Styles

Decorating a bonsai can enhance its visual appeal and add to the overall aesthetic of the display. Adding rocks, stones, or pebbles to the display can help create a natural look and feel for your bonsai. Rocks can also be used to anchor the bonsai in place and provide stability. Similarly, adding moss to the display can help create a sense of age and maturity for your bonsai. Moss can be used to cover the soil, create ground cover, or even create a small, mossy hill for the bonsai to sit on.

Small figurines, such as miniature animals, can be added to the display to create interest and tell a story. Be sure to choose figurines that are in scale with the size of the bonsai and complement the overall style of the display. Elevating the bonsai on a stand or pedestal can help enhance its visual appeal and create a focal point for the display. Choose a stand or pedestal that complements the style and size of the bonsai. Adding small, decorative elements, such as leaves, flowers, or fruit, can help enhance the visual appeal of the bonsai and create a sense of realism. These elements can create a visually appealing and engaging display that showcases the beauty and elegance of your bonsai. Remember to keep the decoration simple and understated so that the focus remains on the bonsai itself.

Chapter 9

Caring for your Bonsai tree according to seasons and climate (indoors and outdoors)

Bonsai care can vary depending on the season and the tree's specific needs. Here's how to look after your bonsai in different seasons:

Spring:

This is a good time to repot your bonsai and add fresh soil. Make sure to choose a soil mix that's appropriate for your tree's needs. Prune any dead or diseased branches and remove any shoots that are growing out of place. It will help promote new growth and maintain the desired shape of the bonsai. You can also fertilize your bonsai with a balanced fertilizer according to the manufacturer's instructions for frequency and amount in order to encourage optimum growth.

Summer:

Bonsai species need more water during the summer to keep up with the increased growth and evaporation. Water your bonsai when the top inch of the soil is dry. Make sure your bonsai is in a location with high humidity. If your home is dry, consider misting the leaves or placing a tray of water near the bonsai. Protect your bonsai from extreme heat, direct sunlight, and harsh winds that can cause stress or damage.

Fall:

As the days get shorter and cooler during autumn, reduce the frequency of watering. This will help the bonsai tree to prepare for winter dormancy. Also, gradually reduce the amount of fertilizer. If temperatures are going to drop below freezing, protect your bonsai by moving it to a warmer location or covering it with a protective cloth.

Winter:

During the winter season, bonsai enter a period of dormancy. This is a time of rest and minimal growth, so there's no need for pruning or fertilization. Watering should be kept to a minimum during the winter. Make sure the soil does not dry out completely but do not water the tree if the soil is still wet.

Chapter 10

Pest, Diseases, and Fungus Control

Insects and pests can attack bonsai trees and cause damage or disease. Here are some common pests to look out for:

Aphids: Small, pear-shaped insects that suck sap from leaves and stems of bonsai trees and cause yellowing and wilting of both leaves and stems and ultimately cause distorted growth.

Mealybugs: they are small, white insects that feed on sap and produce sticky honeydew. They can cause yellowing, wilting, and sooty mold.

Spider mites: These are tiny, red/green pests that feed on plant cells and cause yellow speckling on leaves and fine webs.

Scale insects: Small, hard-shelled insects that feed on sap and can cause yellowing, wilting, and synthesize sticky honeydew.

Borers: Larvae that tunnel into the trunk and branches, causing damage and sometimes killing the tree.

Fungal diseases can be a problem for bonsai trees, causing damage and reducing the plant's overall health and appearance. Here are some common fungal diseases to look out for:

Powdery mildew: A white, powdery growth on leaves and stems that can cause yellowing, stunted growth, and defoliation.

Black spot: Black, circular spots on leaves that can cause yellowing, wilting, and defoliation.

Botrytis: Gray or brown patches on leaves, stems, and flowers that can cause wilting, collapse, and death.

A - How to avoid them (using alcohol, neem oil, pesticides, and insecticides)

To prevent or manage insect, pest, and disease problems, keep the bonsai healthy because a strong, healthy tree is better equipped to resist pests and disease. Inspect your bonsai regularly for signs of pests or disease and act quickly if you find any problems.

For insect/pest control, both alcohol and neem oil can be used to protect your bonsai. Rubbing alcohol can be used to control pests like scale insects, mealybugs, and spider mites. Simply mix equal parts of alcohol and water, and use a cotton swab to apply the solution directly to the pests. Be sure to avoid spraying the alcohol solution on delicate parts of the plant, as it can cause damage.

Neem oil is derived from the neem tree and has insecticidal properties. It can be used to control a wide range of pests, including aphids, mites, and caterpillars. To use neem oil, mix it with water according to the manufacturer's instructions, and spray it directly onto the pests. Be sure to avoid spraying neem oil on hot, sunny days, as it can cause leaf burn. Both alcohol and neem oil can be effective in controlling pests on bonsai, but it's important to remember that they can also be toxic to beneficial insects and other wildlife. Additionally, these substances should be used sparingly and only as needed, as overuse can lead to pesticide resistance and other problems.

B - Dealing with different types of Pests

If you need to use a pesticide, choose one safe for bonsai and follow the manufacturer's instructions carefully. Certain insects, such as ladybugs and green lacewings, feed on pests and can help control populations. If you're bringing a new bonsai into your collection, isolate it for several weeks to ensure it doesn't introduce any pests or diseases. As a pest control method, it's always best to monitor your bonsai regularly and address pest problems early on to minimize damage and maintain the health and beauty of your trees. To prevent or manage fungal diseases, ensure that your bonsai is planted in well-draining soil and is getting adequate light, water, and humidity. Over-watering can create conditions that are ideal for fungal growth. Avoid watering the foliage and keep the surrounding area as dry as possible to reduce the spread of fungal diseases. If you need to use a fungicide, choose one safe for bonsai and follow the manufacturer's instructions carefully. If you find any infected parts, remove and dispose of them promptly to help prevent the spread of fungal diseases.

Chapter 11

Techniques and Strategies to grow Bonsai trees

There are various strategies and techniques that can be used to grow bonsai trees.

- Choose species that are well-suited to the climate and growing conditions in your area. Some species are more tolerant of temperature extremes, and others are better suited for humid or dry conditions.

- Select a container that is appropriate for the size of your bonsai tree and is in proportion to the tree. A container that is too large or too small can detract from the overall appearance of the bonsai.

- Use a well-draining soil mix that is specifically formulated for bonsai. This soil will provide adequate nutrients and moisture for the tree's roots to grow.

- Regular pruning is important for controlling the size and shape of the bonsai tree. Prune branches and leaves that are too long or too thick and also remove any dead or diseased wood.

- Train the branches of the bonsai tree to grow in the desired shape and direction. This may involve the use of wire or other training tools to guide the growth of the branches.

- Bonsai trees require regular watering, but it is important not to over-water, as this can lead to root rot.

- Regular fertilization with a balanced fertilizer will help to promote healthy growth and encourage the development of strong roots and branches.

- Bonsai trees need adequate sunlight exposure to grow properly but be careful not to expose them to too much direct sunlight, as this can cause leaf burn.

By following these tips and care guidelines, you can produce a healthy and beautiful bonsai tree that will thrive for many years to come.

Chapter 12

Additional Information

Bonsai is a traditional art form that originated in Japan. It has been practiced in Japan for over a thousand years and has been passed down from generation to generation. The term "bonsai" is derived from the Japanese words "bon," meaning tray or shallow container, and "sai," meaning plant. Bonsai is the art of growing miniature trees in containers and carefully shaping and training them to achieve the desired aesthetic effect. Bonsai is now popular all over the world and is considered an important part of Japanese culture and heritage. The bonsai world is diverse and encompasses a wide range of styles, techniques, and traditions from different countries and cultures. Bonsai artists, enthusiasts, and organizations from around the world come together to share their knowledge, skills, and experiences through events such as exhibitions, workshops, and competitions. There are numerous bonsai organizations, clubs, and websites dedicated to bonsai, providing resources and information on everything from basic techniques to advanced styles and traditions. Bonsai magazines, books, and videos are also widely available, allowing people to learn about bonsai and stay up-to-date with the latest developments in the bonsai world. In summary, the bonsai world is a vibrant, diverse, and dynamic community of individuals and organizations dedicated to the art, culture, and practice of bonsai.

Bonsai trees have a lifespan similar to that of their full-sized counterparts, and with proper care and attention, they can live for many years and even generations. The lifespan of a bonsai tree depends on various factors, such as the species of tree, the conditions in which it is grown, and the quality of care it receives. In general, bonsai trees that are grown in an environment that closely mimics their natural habitat, with appropriate light, water, and soil conditions, will have a longer lifespan. Regular pruning, training, and repotting will also help maintain the health and vitality of a bonsai tree, allowing it to live a long and productive life. Bonsai trees are living organisms, and like all living things, they will eventually age and die. However, with proper care, a bonsai tree can live for many decades or even centuries, and in some cases, it can be passed down from generation to generation as a treasured family heirloom. In short, bonsai trees have the potential for a long lifespan, and the practice of bonsai is a unique way to create a living work of art that can be enjoyed and appreciated for many years to come.

A - Famous Bonsai Artists in the World

Bonsai is an ancient art form with a rich history and a vibrant contemporary community. Here are some of the world-famous bonsai artists who have made significant contributions to the field:

Masahiko Kimura,

A Japanese bonsai master is known for his innovative style and his ability to create incredibly realistic, expressive bonsai trees.

Yuji Yoshimura,

A Japanese bonsai master who helped to popularize bonsai in the Western world and was instrumental in establishing the International Bonsai Association.

Additional Information

John Y. Naka,
An American bonsai master who was widely regarded as one of the greatest bonsai artists of the 20th century and who helped to establish bonsai as a legitimate art form in the United States.

Daisaku Nomoto,
A Japanese bonsai master known for his exceptional skills in bonsai design and who helped to spread the art of bonsai around the world.

Shinji Suzuki,
A Japanese bonsai master famous for his expertise with large and impressive bonsai trees and who helped to establish the World Bonsai Convention.

These artists and many others have helped to shape the world of bonsai and to inspire new generations of bonsai enthusiasts and artists. Their work continues to be admired and studied, and they have left a lasting legacy in the world of bonsai.

B - Oldest Bonsai Tree

Ancient bonsai trees are symbols of the longevity and beauty of the bonsai art and are admired by bonsai enthusiasts and artists around the world. Japan is widely considered to be the country with the largest number of bonsai specimens and artists. Bonsai has a long history in Japan, dating back over a thousand years, and the country is home to some of the World's finest bonsai collections and exhibitions. The art of bonsai is deeply rooted in

Japanese culture, and many of the techniques and styles used today were developed in Japan.

The exact age of bonsai trees, as many have been passed down through generations is often estimated based on various factors such as size, appearance, and historical records. However, some of the oldest known bonsai trees are said to be over a thousand years old. One of the oldest bonsai trees in the world is **the FICUS bonsai** tree in Parabiago, Italy, assumed to be 1000+ years old. Among them, **WHITE PINE bonsai**, known as "Sandai-Shogun-No-Matsu," is said to be over 500 years old. This tree is housed in the Tokoname Bonsai Museum in Aichi Prefecture, Japan, and is considered a national treasure. Another ancient bonsai is a **Japanese white pine** known as **"Goshin,"** which is estimated to be over 1000 years old. This tree is housed in the Omiya Bonsai Museum in Saitama, Japan, and is considered one of the most valuable and important bonsai trees in the world.

In addition to Japan, there are also large bonsai communities in other countries, including the United States, China, and Europe. Bonsai has gained popularity in recent years, and a large community discovering the joy of growing and nurturing these miniature trees. The art of bonsai continues to evolve and spread around the world, and today, bonsai enthusiasts can be found in countries across the globe. In other countries, such as the United Kingdom and Germany, the bonsai community is smaller but dedicated, with enthusiasts sharing their love of bonsai and learning from one another.

Additional Information

In recent years, bonsai has gained wider recognition and acceptance in Europe and there are now.

Several organizations are dedicated to promoting and preserving the art. **The European Bonsai Association** is one such organization, bringing together bonsai enthusiasts and artists from across the continent to share their knowledge and passion for bonsai. Some countries in Europe, such as Italy and Spain, have a rich tradition of bonsai culture and host several exhibitions and events each year. Europe also boasts several bonsai nurseries and suppliers that provide high-quality trees, tools, and other supplies to bonsai enthusiasts. The growing popularity of bonsai in Europe means that there are many opportunities for enthusiasts to connect with one another, attend workshops and exhibitions, and learn more about this fascinating and rewarding art.

Chapter 13

Conclusion

In conclusion, bonsai is an ancient and fascinating art form that has been practiced for over a thousand years. It involves growing miniature trees in containers and carefully shaping and training them to achieve the desired aesthetic effect. Bonsai has cultural roots in Japan, but it is now popular all over the world, with enthusiasts and practitioners from many countries and cultures. Bonsai trees and the bonsai industry can have significant economic value, and the bonsai world is a vibrant, diverse, and dynamic community that supports the culture and practice of bonsai.

Many people find aesthetic comfort from bonsai, which provides visually pleasing miniature landscapes and has a calming and meditative effect. The focus on nurturing and caring for a living organism can provide a sense of purpose and connection to nature, while the beauty of the finished bonsai can bring a sense of peace and serenity to its observer. In addition, the careful attention to detail required in bonsai cultivation can help to improve one's focus and concentration, while the repetitive tasks involved in bonsai care can provide a sense of structure and routine. Overall, bonsai can offer a unique form of aesthetic comfort that combines the calming effects of nature with the artistic satisfaction of creating a beautiful work of art. Whether grown and tended for personal enjoyment or shared with others, bonsai can bring joy, peace, and a sense of accomplishment to those who engage with this fascinating and rewarding hobby.

Chapter 14

Glossary

A list of terms used in this eBook elaborates as follows:

Accent plant: A small plant displayed next to a bonsai. Accent plants are typically used when a bonsai is formally displayed at a show or exhibition. Accent Plants can include any perennial, bamboo, or grass.

Air Layering: Is a method of propagating bonsai. Layering is more complicated than taking cuttings but has the advantage that the propagated portion can continue to receive water and nutrients from the parent plant while it is forming roots. This is important for plants that form roots slowly or for propagating large pieces.

Akadama

A Japanese volcanic Bonsai soil is ideal for most species of deciduous trees. Generally, the term means red clay balls.

Apex: The highest point of the tree. On a bonsai, this can be a single branch or a series of small branches. It can also be foliage or jin.

Bonsai: Japanese term for the art of cultivating and training a plant to create the illusion of a dwarfed tree. Bonsai is a Japanese word made up of two characters or word phrases, "bon" and "sai ."Bon is pronounced as the English word "bone" and means pot, container, or tray. Sai is pronounced as the English word "sigh" and means tree or plant in Japanese.

Branch bender: A clamp or jack used to bend branches or trunks into a different position.

Branch splitter: Also known as a trunk splitter, this cutting tool is specially designed to split trunks with minimal residual damage.

Chlorosis: A yellowing of leaf tissue due to a lack of chlorophyll. Possible causes of chlorosis include poor drainage, damaged roots, compacted roots, high alkalinity, and nutrient deficiencies in the plant.

Callus: Woody 'scar' tissue that forms over a wound where a branch has been pruned. It's the tree's healing process.

Canopy: The peripheral foliage of the upper branches and those on the outer part of the tree.

Crown: Upper part of a tree where branches spread out from the trunk and define your bonsai silhouette.

Conifer: A tree that bears cones, mainly evergreen trees such as pines, cedars, spruces, and junipers. Coniferous trees have small and waxy leaves, sometimes needles, which are usually kept all year.

Deciduous: A tree that has a seasonal growth cycle where new foliage is produced in the spring, then grows throughout the summer, turns colors in autumn, and drops in the winter, leaving buds on the branches for next spring's new foliage. Deciduous trees enter a state of dormancy annually.

Glossary

Dieback: Death of shoots or branch tips caused by drought, insects, disease, lack of light, or extreme weather conditions.

Defoliation: Leaf pruning, whereby some or all of the leaves are removed to encourage new shoots and smaller leaves, which can greatly increase ramifications.

Dormancy: Is the resting period for bonsai, where little or no growth is produced - usually autumn and winter months.

Dwarf: A variety or cultivar that is smaller than the species tree but retains all of the characteristics of a full-size species tree. Dwarfs are typically compact and slow growing.

Fertilizer: This is "food" for your bonsai, shrubs, and plants, usually comprised of NPK: Phosphorous for the roots, Nitrogen for the foliage, and Potassium for the flowers.

Fungicide: A chemical compound used to prevent the growth and spread of the fungus, which can cause serious damage to a bonsai.

Germination: The process by which a bonsai seed leaves the dormant state starts into growth, developing roots and shoots.

Girth: The circumference of a Bonsai tree measured at its widest point or at just above the root base.

Hair Roots: Fine roots that absorb water and nutrients from the soil.

Humidity: The amount or degree of moisture in the air.

Insecticide: A chemical (synthetic or organic) used to kill or repel insects. There are numerous botanical and mineral powders that are toxic to insects, as well as biodegradable chemicals such as insecticidal soaps.

Loam: A rich soil composed of clay, sand, and organic matter.

NPK: Acronym for the three major bonsai nutrients and used to describe the amounts of each readily available.' N' is for nitrogen,' P' is for phosphorus, and' K' is for potassium.

Needle: A very narrow leaf, often evergreen and usually of a stiff texture, like those found on a pine tree.

Photosynthesis: The process by which plants convert water and carbon dioxide into carbohydrates, using sunlight as the source of energy and the aid of chlorophyll.

pH: Measure of soil acidity or alkalinity. The pH is a measure of the acidity or basicity (alkalinity) of a material when dissolved in water. It is expressed on a scale from 0 to 14. Roughly, pH can be divided into the following ranges:

pH 0-2 Strongly acidic

pH 3-5 Weakly acidic

pH 6-8 Neutral

pH 9-11 Weakly basic

pH 12-14 Strongly basic

Glossary

Pot: A growing container for bonsai, usually high-fired clay. The Chinese or Japanese word bon means "tray" or "shallow pot."

Pruning: The process of controlling the shape and growth rate of a bonsai by cutting back the shoots, stems, and branches.

Raffia: a fiber that originates from the raffia palm used to wrap branches and trunk before bending. It will help reduce the likelihood of splitting branches.

Repotting: The practice of taking a pot-grown bonsai out of its container to refresh the soil and encourage renewed root growth. It's also a great time to select a new or larger pot, and it's imperative to the health of a bonsai.

Rootball: The large mass of roots visible on a bonsai when removed from its pot.

Root pruning: The practice of cutting back the roots when repotting from one pot to another will encourage new root growth and promote future growth.

Rooting hormone: A powder or liquid growth hormone is used to promote the development of roots on a cutting. It's formulated for the propagation of cuttings and stimulates the development of adventitious roots.

Transpiration: A natural process of water loss from the surfaces of plant leaves through stomata and stems.

If you've enjoyed reading this book, subscribe* to my mailing list to get exclusive content and sneak peeks at my future books.

Visit the link below:

http://eepurl.com/glvBjj

OR

Use the QR Code:

(*Must be 13 years or older to subscribe)

Printed in Great Britain
by Amazon